10 WAY

How to Fast-Track Progression Early in Career

10 Tips for Accelerated Career Growth

By

K. Hunter

This book is dedicated to:

Every dreamer. Every person looking out into a competitive world and asking "what can I do to stand out? How can I grow with so much talent surrounding me?" This book is dedicated to your future self and your future success.

Table of Contents

Introduction

We all want to outpace the competition, even when the only competition is ourselves. Most people dream of moving ahead in their careers quickly; to that end, enclosed in these pages you will find ten tips for fast-tracking progress early in your career. You see, the difficulty of getting ahead in work is that at times, it needs to be both a marathon and a sprint. Most people will work for 30+ years (marathon) but will also work very hard every day (sprint). Implementing the ten tips found in this book will have you on the fast track to outpacing your competition and completing your five to ten-year goals. But remember, action is required to make your dream a reality!

Section One: Simplify Your Life, Make Room for the Obsession

One day, I was reading a magazine when I stumbled across an article claiming that most successful people had simplified their daily clothing choices to conserve their decision-making "juice" for the rest of the day. At the time, I didn't buy it, and neither did most people. How could the fifteen minutes spent deciding what to wear impact my decision-making capacity for the next twenty-four hours? It was not until I was twenty-nine years old and recreating my wardrobe that I realized the magnitude of this power move. By having a weeks' worth of professional attire (neutral colors) laid out in one place, I was able to pick my outfit in the morning without having to make a choice. *Grab and go* (except the mantra applied here was of the money saving kind, unlike a Starbuck's habit). The clothing began picking me, and that is when I learned how this colored all aspects of my day. If you only allow acceptable options into your life, any choice you make will be a good one.

This minimalization concept is no longer foreign to us. We have all heard the mantras calling for us to declutter our spaces and minds. Let me add my own voice to that chorus. At first, I was as disappointed as you are. "You mean to tell me that I won't feel better if I buy another pair of shoes or a second car or color-coded pairs of headphones?" I am sorry to say, that is exactly what I am telling you. With each unnecessary item comes an unnecessary decision. The concept of intellectual energy conservation doesn't stop at material goods: we need to prioritize our time. We must learn to say no to things that do not propel us forward and yes to things that push us out of our comfort zone. We need to relearn how to prioritize. Notice I did not say "reprioritize," but "relearn"—the entire process. Our foundation is broken. We have been conditioned to prioritize based on what is currently important to us and those around us. We live in the now and desire immediate gratification. We must relearn how to correctly prioritize to achieve our goals, regardless of the timeline or commitment. You are not giving up on an essential priority when you say you cannot go to a social event. You are not giving up on a priority if you miss a movie release today in order to teach yourself a new skill instead. Your decision-making capability and brain power should be allocated for professional and growth-enhancing decisions. Save your energy, and in the end, it will propel your growth. This, my friend, is when the obsession is born.

Now, you may ask what you will be doing with all this decision-making juice I speak of. Decide what you want to do with your life! Decide what career you want, what professional field you enjoy, what your career progression should look like, and then visualize your optimal goals. Start building a vision of your truest desires, and start making the decisions necessary to lay a strong foundation.

Section Two: Leave Your Ego at the Door

This is going to be a bumpy ride that includes a lot of mistakes, failures, learning, and feedback. It will always be necessary to leave your ego at the door. When I go for a run, I hype myself up by listening to a commencement speech made by Denzel Washington, who references "falling forward" instead of having a plan to fall back on. The point here is not to be afraid of mistakes. You will make mistakes while striving to do better—we all do. How you handle those mistakes and the next steps you take will define your progress.

So, you've made a mistake—now what? Maybe you tried to remedy an issue on your own that was above your head. Maybe you tried to prove that an outside-of-the-box method would work, and it didn't. The first step: own your failure. Take responsibility for the results (or lack thereof). This will help provide the space to evaluate what went wrong and proactively troubleshoot the issue in the future. You cannot begin to improve on a failure if you cannot admit one has occurred.

Secondly, make a list of the learning opportunities that have come from this mistake. At the very least, you learned that this approach did not help. Did you learn what could work? Did you find the pain point in the method you used? Did you learn how others did not react well to the idea you proposed? Did you move too quickly or not quickly enough? Keep progress notes for your next attempt at greatness.

Finally, be prepared to receive and use feedback. This is where the ability to admit mistakes becomes important: you get the opportunity to take feedback from those around you and reflect on the feedback provided. Feedback can come from a superior, a peer, a client, or a customer. Where the feedback comes from does not matter if the feedback helps you grow. Be open to suggestions and the advice you are given—it may include information that will help perfect your technique. If you are unable to admit your failure, you will be unable to use it to grow and learn. Leaving your ego at the door opens many more doors in the long run.

Section Three: Speak Less, Listen More (at First)

There's a famous quote that gets passed around the business advice world: "if you are the smartest person in the room, then you need to find a new room." There is a second important point to be made here. You can surround yourself with the smartest people you know, but if you do not stop to listen and learn from them, their value is wasted. Especially in the beginning of your career, be a sponge. Actively listen and retain all you can. The information you absorb and the decisions you witness may not always be the best, but you will always learn a lesson. You will learn the best way to do things—or the way you do not want to do things in the future. At some point in your career, it will be time to speak up, but that is not when you are first starting out. As a novice, you want to learn from the experience of others and leverage the knowledge they can provide. Take notes. Write everything down.

The one caveat to speaking less is that you should ask questions. However, ensure you are in the right setting. For example, if you are provided an opportunity to sit in on a meeting with business leaders and they are discussing an important project or initiative, that is not the right time to ask questions. Take note of your questions as you think of them; then, after the meeting, ask your superior if you can setup a debrief to go over those points you did not understand. This is not only a more appropriate setting, but it also conveys that you are eager to learn and are looking to understand more about the organization. Trust me, this will stand out to your superior and they will not forget it.

Section Four: Say Yes to Everything, Then Go Learn It

There are many times in life a boss will need work completed that no one knows how to do—formulas in Excel, a toolkit created in Microsoft Word, etc. When this happened to me, it was about a formula in Excel I did not know how to use. I told myself I could learn. I raised my hand and said, "I don't know how, but tonight I will figure it out."

YouTube can be your best friend for this. There are thousands of YouTube videos on every topic you can imagine. YouTube has taught me more about Microsoft Suite than any peer or superior I have ever had. Take every assignment you can in the beginning, even if you are not comfortable with it. Just be honest when accepting it: tell your boss that this is the first time you've attempted such a project, but you would like the opportunity to try. This is how you jump on the fast track to a promotion. Using this tactic not only helps your boss and shows them that you are eager and willing to learn, but also teaches you an invaluable amount of information in the process. You may end up with more work than your counterparts at times. You may end up with extra projects and assignments and will be working harder than others, but when the time comes for one person to receive the promotion, it will be you.

Section Five: Use Your Resources

In the last section, we talked about using YouTube videos to learn new skills. This is just one example of a resource you may have at your fingertips. Now, we all have different resources available to us, but we also have different methods for gaining more resources.

The most important lesson in this section is to never waste a resource. If you have access to a computer and an internet connection, use the free tutorials you can find online. Google can teach you a tremendous amount about any profession. Look for websites and professional organizations that are offering free webinars and courses. If you do not have a computer, your local library (many of which provide computer access) can be just as valuable.

The people you work with are also a resource. Lean on your colleagues. This also coincides with the tip from earlier about leaving your ego at the door. Pick the brain of a peer who has been at your organization longer than you. The more you leverage those around you, peers and leaders alike, the better off you will be.

If you hit it off with someone who has been in the profession longer than you (maybe you joke around in the coffee room, maybe you performed well at a meeting they attended), ask them to be your mentor! This can be scary at first. What if they say no? Won't that be embarrassing? Do not worry about that—most people will be honored by the request. They may say no based on time and availability, but will be tickled that you asked and will hold you in high regard for having the confidence and knowledge to do so. Trust me—the more you ask for, the more you will receive.

Section Six: Learn to Speak Up

So you've made room for your ambition and interest. You've begun to use the resources available to you and have been listening and learning for some time. Now it is time to stand out.

Find a way to make your presence known at the right times. Now that you have learned from listening to the leaders around you, make a statement when it is appropriate. When you are in a meeting with your peers and superiors, politely give your recommendation (after detailed planning). Come into work with an idea for a new initiative or project and pitch it to your boss in private. If you are lucky enough to have found a mentor, practice establishing your presence with them and understanding the difference between helpful interjections and interruptions that will leave others feeling put off. When you are early in your career, it may not be the best idea to disagree with a business leader in a public forum or insult a project a peer is working on (even if you are sure you are right), but it *is* the right time to make recommendations to your superiors and begin soft-pitching ideas.

Section Seven: Ask for More, Do the "Unnecessary"

While the previous sections have been focused on tips and advice to help you progress quickly through the early stages of your career, this section focuses on the hustle. This section is a reminder that there is no replacement for hard work. There is only the advantage you will have by coupling hard work with the intentional actions listed in this booklet.

You will notice early on that not everyone in your organization or on your team works the same amount. Some people stay late and arrive early while others walk in on time, and others may even arrive late. Some are completing extra projects and pitching new ideas constructed over the weekend while others simply complete the mandatory work assigned to them. We call doing the bare minimum "checking the box." These employees do enough work to keep their jobs and to complete everything asked of them.

There is nothing wrong with this approach if you are satisfied staying at the same level for many, many years. But you have greater ambition and more potential than that. Do not waste your potential! Put in the effort and you will fly past those individuals before you even realize it's happening. Always volunteer for projects, and if possible, work on initiatives in your free time that will help propel the team forward.

This is not sustainable forever—it will cut into other aspects of your life. However, if you can develop a reputation for going above and beyond early on, it will pay off ten-fold over the next few years.

Section Eight: Create Worth

In the prior section, I spoke about going the extra mile—putting in the extra work. This section focuses on the type of work you spend your free time on.

We all have work we must do but don't love. If you love every aspect of your job, you are one of the luckiest people in the world. For the rest of us, we must complete certain menial tasks that we would rather give up in a heartbeat. Ensure these are not the type of tasks you are completing voluntarily in your free time. When you go the extra mile and put in extra time for work, ensure those projects are creating worth. You want to be sure that you are showing your boss a worth within you they did not know existed. This is how you move to the next level.

If you are going to decide to work voluntarily on nights and weekends, don't organize your boss's papers or the office closet. Take an existing process and find a way to make it better. Take a slow process and make it more efficient. Take a broken process and fix it.

Better yet, identify an issue your boss has not realized exists and propose a brand-new approach. These are the types of initiatives that will demonstrate your worth in the long run.

Section Nine: Document Your Progress

Now that you are focusing your time and energy on standing out, volunteering for projects, and developing better, more efficient ways of completing work, you need to ensure you are documenting your progress. I once had a boss tell me to keep a "kudos" folder—some of the best advice I have ever been given. Keep a folder (whether physical or digital) of all your important work successes.

Many times, when you help another employee or make their life easier in one way or another, they will send you a thank-you email. Save every one of these. One day, you will be able to use these items to pitch your promotion.

Section Ten: Package Your Worth

Moving up the ranks, getting raises and promotions, all depends upon the value you can bring to your boss and your organization. It is not simply about the work you do, but the value you create.

If your company is compensating correctly, then your pay will be based on the value you bring. Using the first nine sections of this book, you have learned how to develop, showcase, and document this value for when the time comes to speak about a promotion, raise, etc. Whatever your ask may be, you must be able to demonstrate your value when you make it. Therefore, packaging your worth is of the upmost importance.

Hopefully, you listened to the advice in Section 9 and have saved your important works and any notes of gratitude you have received from others. When it is time to speak with your boss about taking the next step in your career, come with a presentation—a humble, fact-based, straightforward document that lists all your accomplishments at the organization. This should be relatively easy if you've been tracking everything. Add an appendix to the document with screenshots of the notes of gratitude and thanks you received from others in the organization. Being presented with this combination of successful, important work you have completed and the demonstrated impact you have had on others will make it hard for them not to promote you or give you that raise you have been waiting for!

The last note here is to deliver this as you would deliver a book report. This is not a bragging session but rather an evidence-driven argument for why your value has surpassed your status vis-à-vis title or salary at the organization. If you have an intuitive boss, they will likely see the conversation coming and will welcome a discussion of your career aspirations and what, if anything, you need to do to move to the next level—or, they will agree that you are already there!

Conclusion

Being early in your career has its advantages. Usually, you have fewer outside commitments, more energy, and more room to learn. Use this time to learn, to grow, to take risks with great reward potential, and to work your butt off! If you implement the recommendations made in this booklet, they will pay off and you will quickly outpace your competition. Remember, for better or worse, sometimes you are running both a marathon *and* a sprint. Good luck!

About the Author

K. Hunter was born in May of 1991 and is based in the United States. The author holds a master's degree in Industrial & Organizational Psychology from Hofstra University as well as numerous professional certifications specific to the field of Human Resources. Hunter has been expeditiously promoted at her past three organizations of employment. Additional experience includes cofounding a not-for-profit corporation with a focus on helping children from disadvantaged populations.